STRATEGIC ALLIANCES MANAGEMENT

KEY TO SUCCESS

ERIC SNETHKAMP

Eric Snethkamp

https://www.linkedin.com/in/ericsnethkamp/

ISBN 9798387391071 (Paperback Edition)

Published March 2023

Published by Eric Snethkamp

To my beautiful wife and best friend, Michele.

My source of happiness and motivation.

Contents

CHAPTER ONE

INTRODUCTION

Welcome to the world of strategic alliances and partnerships! In today's rapidly changing business landscape, it's becoming increasingly important for organizations to establish mutually beneficial relationships with other companies to gain a competitive advantage. Strategic alliances can be incredibly valuable, allowing companies to share resources, knowledge, and expertise to achieve common goals. But managing these relationships is not always easy. They require careful planning, communication, and effort from all parties involved.

"Partnering has proven itself one of the most powerful business tools for dealing with fast-changing markets, technologies, and customers. As the global economy speeds up, partnering is becoming the weapon of choice for today's successful competitors." - Curtis E. Sahakian

This book is designed to serve as a guide to managing the key focus areas of strategic alliances. Each key focus area could be dissected, investigated, analyzed, and prescribed in great depth. The scope of this book is to highlight what they are and what the alliance leader should consider while managing the alliance. There are many ways to take deeper dives into each key focus area, including my Linkedin posts and other resources that I will share with you at the end of the book.

The job of being an alliance leader necessitates being well-versed and capable in managing a complex array of business, personal and cultural skills. In the following pages, you'll find practical suggestions and strategies for effectively managing these complex relationships. Whether you're an executive leader, a strategic alliance manager, or someone simply interested in learning more about this topic, I will share the areas to focus on and tips you need to succeed.

CHAPTER TWO

WHAT ARE STRATEGIC ALLIANCES?

Purpose

A strategic alliance is a formal agreement between two or more companies to work together in a mutually beneficial manner. Typically, a strategic alliance aims to achieve a specific objective or set of objectives, such as increasing market share, reducing costs, or improving efficiency. Achieving those objectives can cover a very broad range of activities and management focus areas, including sharing resources, knowledge, and expertise, collaborating on research and development, marketing, sales and distribution activities, and much more. Just about every aspect of operating a business is mirrored in operating a successful strategic alliance. The results are that strategic alliances can take many different forms, including joint ventures, partnerships, licensing agreements, and marketing agreements.

Strategic alliances offer many benefits for the partner companies, including increased market reach, shared resources and knowledge, reduced costs, and increased competitiveness. Strategic alliances also come with risks, such as ruined relationships, damage to reputations, and negative financial impacts. It's important to carefully consider the goals and objectives of a strategic alliance and balance those against the compatibility of the companies involved and their appetites for risk and reward.

Effective strategic alliances require strong communication, trust, and mutual respect between partners to mitigate the risks and maximize the rewards. It is also important to have a clear understanding of the roles and responsibilities of each partner, as well as the terms and conditions of the agreement. Additionally, companies must be willing to invest the time and resources necessary to manage and maintain the alliance to ensure its success. Overall, strategic alliances can be a powerful tool for companies looking to grow and compete in today's business environment *with* the appropriate levels of commitment and management.

The goals or purposes of strategic alliances can vary depending on the specific needs and objectives of each company or companies involved in the alliance. Common goals and purposes may include:

To expand market reach:

One of the most common purposes of strategic alliances is to expand the reach of each of the companies involved in the alliance. This is achieved by accessing new customers, entering new markets, or increasing visibility and/or sales in existing markets.

A good example is the partnership between Coca-Cola and McDonald's. Their alliance was formed in the 1980s and has been instrumental in expanding both companies' reach. Coca-Cola has been the exclusive soft drink provider for McDonald's restaurants worldwide, and McDonald's has been one of Coca-Cola's largest customers. Coca-Cola has been able to tap into McDonald's extensive global network, and McDonald's has been able to offer its customers a high-quality and well-known beverage brand. Their alliance has been so successful that it has lasted for several decades and continues to be a key part of both companies' growth strategies.

To leverage strengths and resources:

Companies can leverage the strengths and resources of their partners to become more competitive, improve their product offerings, customer experiences, and increase profitability.

ActiveCampaign is a customer experience automation platform that helps businesses create and manage customer journeys, while Salesforce is a leading customer relationship management (CRM) platform.

By forming a strategic alliance and integrating their capabilities, the two companies were able to offer businesses a complete solution for managing customer engagement, marketing automation, sales, and customer service and helped businesses improve their customer experiences, drive sales growth and increase operational efficiency.

The result for customers was a single platform to manage their customer engagement and sales processes, reducing the need for multiple tools and platforms. This made it easier for businesses to access the information they needed to make data-driven decisions and improve their overall performance.

To share risk and cost:

By sharing the risk and cost of developing new products or entering new markets, companies can reduce their financial exposure and increase their chances of success.

In 2017, Procter & Gamble and Amazon formed a strategic alliance aimed at improving the e-commerce experience for P&G customers. Through the partnership, P&G was able to leverage Amazon's vast e-commerce platform, which helped reduce its distribution costs and risks associated with selling its products online.

Amazon benefited from the partnership by gaining access to P&G's vast product portfolio and customer base, which helped it expand its product offerings and reach more customers. The partnership also allowed Amazon to reduce its risks and costs associated with product fulfillment and delivery.

All-in-all, the partnership between P&G and Amazon benefited both companies by helping share risks and costs associated with expanding their e-commerce presence.

To access new technologies and knowledge:

Strategic alliances can provide companies access to new technologies and knowledge they may not have had otherwise, which can help them improve their products and increase their competitiveness.

The partnership between IBM and Apple serves as an example. The alliance was formed in 2014 to bring IBM's enterprise solutions and services to the Apple iOS platform. IBM brought its expertise in cloud computing, big data, and mobile security to the table, while Apple brought its cutting-edge hardware and user-friendly software.

This alliance allowed IBM to tap into Apple's expertise in design, engineering, and user experience, while also giving Apple access to IBM's vast technology and business expertise. The partnership also allowed IBM to expand its reach into new markets, such as healthcare and retail, through the development of industry-specific mobile solutions. The alliance has proven to be a win-win for both companies, with IBM reporting significant growth in its cloud business and Apple reporting increased enterprise sales.

To increase revenue and profitability:

By leveraging the strengths and resources of their partners, expanding their reach, and improving their competitiveness, companies can increase their revenue and profitability.

Another Apple example, this time Apple Inc. and AT&T. In 2007, Apple introduced the iPhone and entered into an exclusive agreement with AT&T to be the sole provider of wireless services for the phone. This alliance allowed Apple to access AT&T's large customer base and expand its market reach. It also allowed AT&T to offer its customers a unique and innovative product, thereby increasing its revenue and profitability. The alliance between Apple and AT&T was so successful that it became one of the largest revenue-generating partnerships for both companies.

To strengthen brand image and reputation:

Strategic alliances can help companies strengthen their brand image and reputation by associating themselves with well-respected partners.

Surprise another Apple example. In 2006, Nike and Apple formed a strategic alliance to develop Nike+, a platform that allowed runners to track their performance using the Nike+ sensor and Apple's iPod.

The partnership helped Nike strengthen its brand image as a leader in innovative and high-performance athletic wear and equipment. It also helped Apple gain recognition in the fitness market, as the company had previously been known primarily for its technology products.

The partnership helped companies improve their reputation in the market. Nike was recognized for its innovative products and cutting-edge technology, while Apple was seen as a forward-thinking company invested in the health and wellness industry.

CHAPTER THREE

VARIOUS DEFINITIONS OF STRATEGIC ALLIANCES AND PARTNERSHIPS

In addition to Strategic Alliances, there are a variety of additional "alliance" or "partner" styles of relationships with various definitions. In many cases, these definitions are mixed and mingled to suit the desired outcomes of the entities involved and tend to be very flexible depending upon where you look or whom you ask.

Joint venture:

A joint venture is a business relationship in which two or more companies join together to undertake a specific project or investment. The partners in a joint venture share the risk, costs, and rewards of the project and pool their resources, knowledge, and expertise to achieve a common goal. Joint ventures can take many forms, such as a merger, acquisition, or strategic partnership, and are often established to expand market reach, access new technologies, or enter into new markets.

A joint venture can also result in two or more organizations forming a new company to pursue a specific business opportunity. Joint ventures typically involve sharing ownership, profits, and control of the new company.

Partnership:

A partnership is a type of strategic alliance in which two or more organizations work together to achieve common goals. Partnerships often involve sharing resources, knowledge, and expertise but do not typically involve creating a new company or sharing ownership.

The typical goal of a B2B partnership is to create a mutually beneficial relationship that helps both companies grow and succeed. They can take many forms including licensing, marketing, and distribution agreements.

B2B partnerships/strategic alliances are especially popular in the technology, healthcare, and manufacturing industries.

Consortium:

A consortium is a type of strategic alliance in which two or more organizations pool their resources and expertise to achieve a common goal. Consortiums are often used to fund research and development projects or to pool resources for large-scale projects.

Inter-firm collaboration:

As with other forms of strategic alliances, Inter-firm collaboration refers to the process of working together between two or more organizations to achieve a common goal. This can involve sharing resources, knowledge, and expertise and can take the form of strategic alliances, partnerships, joint ventures, or consortia.

Strategic networks:

Once again, primarily just another name for a strategic alliance; strategic networks refer to the relationships between organizations that are formed for the purpose of achieving a common goal. They can take many forms, including strategic alliances, partnerships, joint ventures, and consortia.

Cooperative agreements:

Co-ops, or cooperative businesses, are owned and operated by a group of companies or individuals who work together to achieve a common goal. They are often focused on providing goods and services to members and they typically operate based on democratic principles such as one member, one vote.

Co-ops can take many forms including consumer co-ops, worker co-ops, producer co-ops, and housing co-ops. They are often established to provide a more affordable or accessible alternative to traditional businesses and to promote community-based economic development.

They are found in many sectors, including agriculture, retail, banking, and housing.

Chapter Four

Strategic Alliance Leaders

Building a strong and effective strategic alliance team is crucial, to say the least. However, strategic alliance executive leaders and managers are a special group of people and are not always easy to identify. They must be good at almost every aspect of operating and leading a business. All without much fanfare or authority and little recognition in return. Considering the range of people and personalities involved in effectively managing an alliance, personal communication skills are critical. Strategic alliance managers have been put in the position of therapist more than once. Focus areas to consider:

Define roles and responsibilities:

Clearly define the roles and responsibilities of each team member, including the lead person for the alliance, the primary point of contact, and the key decision-makers.

Select the right team members:

Choose team members with the necessary skills and expertise and who have a strong commitment to the alliance's success. Consider their experience, skills, and strengths when making selections. Typically, the skills needed to successfully navigate and manage strategic alliances include relationship building, negotiation, strategic thinking, business acumen, cross-cultural communication, people management and the abilities to be flexible and adaptable. Reviewing online job descriptions placed by companies in your industry serve as a great starting point. More on what skills to look for later in the book.

Foster communication and collaboration:

Encourage open and effective communication and collaboration between team members. This will help to ensure that information is shared effectively and that everyone is working toward a common goal.

Establish clear processes and procedures:

Establish clear processes and procedures for decision-making, communication and problem-solving within the team. This helps ensure that everyone is aware of their roles and responsibilities and can work effectively together.

- Define how decisions are made: Establish the alliance's decision-making process first. This should include a clear understanding of who has the power to make decisions, what decisions need to be approved or discussed with other stakeholders and when decisions need to be made.

- Create a communication plan: A communication strategy should define the techniques, frequency and channels used to communicate inside the alliance. Also, it should specify who is in charge of informing the team of updates and changes as well as how problems are identified and resolved.

- Develop a framework for problem-solving: Build a detailed plan for resolving disputes inside the alliance. This should incorporate a method for classifying issues according to importance, deciding who is responsible for fixing each one and establishing success parameters.

- Process and procedure standardization: For important areas like project management, risk management, and financial management, establish standard processes and procedures. This will guarantee that everyone on the team is on the same page regarding how these procedures should be carried out.

- Include stakeholders: All stakeholders should be included in the creation of these processes and procedures. This will make sure that everyone understands their duties and responsibilities and is working from the same page.

- Document everything: Provide clear and simple documentation of all processes and procedures. This covers frameworks for problem-solving, communication plans, decision-making protocols, and established processes and procedures. Ensure that all team members may easily access these materials.

- Review and update regularly: To make sure that these processes and procedures are still applicable and efficient, they should be reviewed and updated on a regular basis. To find opportunities for improvement, get input from the team's stakeholders.

Encourage continuous improvement:

Encourage the team to continuously assess its performance and identify areas for improvement. Regular performance reviews can help identify areas for improvement and allow team members to learn and grow.

Foster a positive and supportive culture:

Foster a positive and supportive culture within the team. Help team members be supportive of each other and to work together to achieve the goals of the alliance. For instance:

1. Communicate effectively: Open and transparent communication is key in strategic alliances. Encourage team members to share their thoughts and ideas and actively listen to their feedback. Be sure to provide regular updates on team goals, progress and changes to keep everyone informed.

2. Celebrate successes: Recognize and celebrate team and individual achievements. This can be as simple as a shout-out in a team or alliance meeting.

3. Encourage collaboration: Encourage team members to work together and share their expertise. This helps build a sense of community and can lead to more innovative solutions.

4. Provide opportunities for growth and development: Support your team members' career growth by providing opportunities for professional development and promotion. This demonstrates your investment in their success and helps build loyalty and engagement.

The role of a strategic alliance executive leader

Strategic Alliance Leaders - "These leaders live in limbo, with little official power and ambiguous roles. Their jobs can be lonely outposts in many cases. They must be the internal advocate, external promoter, chief relationship builder, and master of personal influence. Their job is to identify the strategic value proposition between the companies and,

*at the end of the day, to be able to cultivate sponsors on both sides." -
Steve Steinhilber*

A strategic alliance executive leader plays a critical role in
guiding and overseeing the development and implementation of
strategic alliances. The primary responsibilities of a strategic alliance
executive leader include:

Setting the strategic vision:

The strategic alliance executive leader sets the vision and direction
for the organization's strategic alliance efforts and ensures that they
align with the organization's overall goals and objectives.

Building and managing teams:

The strategic alliance executive leader is responsible for building
and managing the team and ensuring they have the resources and
support they need to succeed.

Overseeing negotiations and management:

The strategic alliance executive leader oversees the negotiations
and management of the alliances and ensures that they are running
smoothly and delivering value to the organization.

Driving growth and innovation:

The strategic alliance executive leader is responsible for driving
growth and innovation through strategic alliances and leveraging
these partnerships to create new opportunities for the organization.

Managing risk and conflict:

The strategic alliance executive leader is responsible for managing
risks and conflicts that may arise during the alliance and ensuring
that they are addressed in a manner that protects the organization's
interests and, when possible, maintain the alliance.

To succeed in this role, a strategic alliance executive leader should
have a strong understanding of the industry and market trends and a
deep understanding of the organization's goals and objectives. They
should also possess excellent leadership and communication skills
and the ability to think critically and make sound business decisions.

The role of a Strategic Alliance Manager

*"Alliance managers are like social chameleons. These leaders have to be
great communicators who are able to talk to everyone from the janitor*

to the CEO. It takes a special breed of person to develop and manage relationships at this level." - Steve Steinhilber

A strategic alliance manager plays a critical role in managing and implementing strategic alliances. These managers are sometimes formally trained however, in many circumstances they are recruited into these roles from positions that help strategic alliance managers develop the necessary skills. Positions such as channel manager, project manager, sales, sales leadership and business consulting. A strategic alliances manager's primary responsibilities include:

Identifying and pursuing new strategic alliance opportunities:

Identifying and evaluating new strategic alliance opportunities that align with the organization's goals and objectives.

Negotiating and managing alliances:

Negotiating the terms of the alliance agreement and managing the day-to-day operations of the alliance to ensure that it is running smoothly.

Communicating and collaborating with partners:

Communicating and collaborating with partners to ensure that everyone is aligned and working toward the same goals.

Measuring and reporting results:

Tracking and reporting on the results of the alliance and using this information to make improvements and drive growth.

Managing risks and conflicts:

Identifying and managing risks and conflicts that may arise during the alliance and finding ways to resolve these issues in a mutually beneficial manner.

Skills to be a Good Strategic Alliance Manager

A good strategic alliance manager should have the following qualities:

Strong Communication Skills:

Ability to communicate effectively with internal and external shareholders. This includes being able to negotiate and manage conflicts.

Strategic Thinking:

Ability to think critically and strategically about the potential benefits and risks of a partnership and make informed decisions to develop long-term strategies for success

Negotiation:

Strong negotiation skills to negotiate agreements, terms, and conditions with partners.

Project management:

The ability to manage projects and ensure that they are delivered on time and within budget is crucial.

Financial acumen:

A good understanding of finance, budgeting, and cost analysis.

Analytical skills:

The ability to analyze data and market trends to make informed decisions.

Relationship building:

The ability to build and maintain strong relationships with partners.

Cultural sensitivity:

Understanding the cultural differences between partners and being able to navigate them is important.

Adaptability:

The ability to adapt to changing market conditions and new technologies.

Legal knowledge:

Understand the legal aspects of contracts, agreements, and negotiations.

CHAPTER FIVE

MANAGING STRATEGIC ALLIANCES

As you've seen to this point, strategic alliances can help organizations achieve greater reach, economies of scale, and faster results than they would achieve on their own. Effective management of strategic alliances is crucial for ensuring that these collaborative agreements deliver the desired results and benefits.

"Developing a solid alliance design is an art, a science, and a craft. It is an art because it requires creativity and because each alliance is a unique creation: no two alliances are the same. It is a science because getting it right requires knowledge about proven recipes. It is a craft because organizations get better at combining art and science when their experience with alliances increases." - Ard-Pieter DeMan

To effectively manage a strategic alliance, leaders need to understand the following key components:

Strategic planning:

It is important to have a clear understanding of the goals and objectives of the alliance, as well as a plan for achieving those goals.

Partner selection:

Careful selection of alliance partners is critical to the success of the alliance. Leaders should assess potential partners based on various factors, including compatibility, expertise, and past performance. More on this in the next section.

Contract negotiation:

Once a partner has been selected, leaders should negotiate a comprehensive contract that defines the terms and conditions of the alliance.

Communication and collaboration:

Communication and collaboration are key components of effective strategic alliance management. Leaders should establish clear lines of communication and put processes in place to foster collaboration between partners.

Performance measurement:

Leaders should establish metrics and KPIs to measure the alliance's performance and identify improvement areas.

Conflict resolution:

Conflicts are inevitable in any collaborative relationship. Leaders should be prepared to manage conflicts effectively and resolve them to benefit all parties. More on this in the upcoming sections.

Continual improvement:

Strategic alliances are dynamic relationships that evolve over time. Leaders should continually assess the performance of the alliance and make changes as needed to ensure its continued success.

Potential pitfalls with strategic alliances

Strategic alliances can be beneficial for companies, but they also come with many potential pitfalls that should be considered before entering into a partnership. Some of the most common pitfalls include:

Misaligned goals and objectives:

If the partners in a strategic alliance have different goals and objectives, it can lead to conflict and, ultimately, the failure of the partnership.

Lack of trust:

Without trust, it can be difficult for partners to work together effectively and resolve conflicts when they arise.

Communication breakdowns:

Poor communication can lead to misunderstandings and misinterpretations, which can cause problems in a strategic alliance.

Inadequate governance:

If the partners do not have clear guidelines for managing the alliance and making decisions, it can lead to confusion and disagreements.

Over-reliance on the alliance:

Companies may become overly reliant on the strategic alliance, limiting their ability to act independently and pursue new opportunities.

Inadequate resources:

If one partner does not have the necessary resources to support the alliance, it can cause problems and lead to the failure of the partnership.

Competition:

If the partners are also competitors, it can be difficult to manage the balance between cooperation and competition, which can cause problems in the alliance.

Acknowledging and minding these potential pitfalls and taking steps to mitigate them is vital to help increase the chances of success in strategic alliances.

CHAPTER SIX

FIRST THINGS FIRST: HOW TO FIND AND FORM STRATEGIC ALLIANCES

Screening and selection of strategic alliances is an important process as the success of the alliance depends on the compatibility of the partners. By taking the time to evaluate potential partners and ensuring that they meet the desired criteria organizations can increase their chances of success in their strategic alliance.

Define criteria:

The first step is to define the criteria that will be used to evaluate potential partners. This may include financial stability, compatibility with the company's culture and values, market expertise, and alignment with the company's goals and objectives.

Identify potential partners:

Consider companies that complement your business in terms of size, product or service offerings, industry, and target markets. Look for partners that have a similar culture and values to your business and that have a good reputation.

Research potential partners:

Research potential partners that align wit your business goals by gathering information from various sources including their website, annual reports, industry publications, and other relevant sources. This can include recommendations from industry experts, understanding their competitors and information from trade events and conferences as well as networking in the same circles.

Evaluate potential partners:

Evaluate potential partners based on the defined criteria and compare the information gathered from the research to determine which partners best fit the alliance.

Vetting strategic alliance partners is an important step in ensuring that an alliance is formed with the right partner and that it has a high likelihood of success. It is critical to conduct due diligence by verifying information about the potential partner including their financial stability, reputation and track record. It may involve contacting references and speaking with other companies that have worked with the potential partner.

Review business goals and objectives:

Evaluate the potential partners' goals and objectives to ensure they align with your own. This will help to ensure that both partners are working toward a common goal.

Evaluate past performance:

Review the potential partners' past performance and track record to assess their ability to deliver on their commitments. Look for a partner with a proven track record of delivering high-quality products or services, meeting deadlines and working well with other organizations.

Assess organizational fit:

Evaluate the potential partners' organizational structure, culture and values to ensure they are a good fit for your organization. A good organizational fit will help facilitate a smooth and effective working relationship.

Review financial stability:

Assess the financial stability of the potential partner. Look for a partner with a strong financial position and the ability to invest in the alliance over the long-term.

Evaluate technology compatibility:

Review the technology and systems used by the potential partner to ensure that they are compatible with your own. A smooth integration of systems and processes can play a major role in the operation and information sharing processes in a strategic alliance.

Evaluate legal and regulatory compliance:

Ensure that the potential partner complies with all relevant legal and regulatory requirements and has a good track record of compliance.

Seek references:

Ask for references from the potential partner and speak with current and past customers and partners to get a better understanding of their work and reputation.

Secure internal company buy-in

Internal company buy-in refers to the level of support and commitment from all levels of a company's employees, management and stakeholders toward a strategic alliance. This involves ensuring that all relevant parties within the company understand and agree with the goals and objectives of the alliance and are motivated to work toward its success.

Having internal company buy-in is important because it can help ensure that the alliance runs smoothly with everyone working together toward a common goal. It can also help ensure that resources and support are made available to the alliance when needed and can help mitigate resistance to change or objections to the alliance.

To achieve internal company buy-in it is important to communicate the benefits of the alliance to all relevant parties and to provide regular updates on its progress. It's also important to involve relevant stakeholders in the planning and implementation of the alliance.

Negotiate and sign the agreement:

After selecting a potential partner, negotiate the terms of the agreement and sign the agreement when both parties are in agreement.

Negotiate terms:

This includes defining the goals and objectives of the alliance, outlining responsibilities and expectations and determining how you will work together.

Draft the agreement:

Create a written agreement that clearly outlines the terms of the alliance. This agreement should be legally binding and include provisions for dispute resolution, termination and renewal.

Contracts

A strategic alliance contract is a legal agreement between two or more organizations that outlines the terms and conditions of their strategic alliance. It is a critical component of any strategic alliance as it sets the expectations and obligations of both partners and provides a framework for resolving disputes. Some key elements of a strategic alliance contract are:

Purpose:

The purpose of the strategic alliance including the goals and objectives of the alliance, the products or services to be developed or delivered and the target markets.

Roles and responsibilities:

The roles and responsibilities of both partners including the resources to be provided, the activities to be performed and the decision-making processes.

Duration:

The duration of the strategic alliance including the start and end dates and any provisions for renewing or terminating the alliance.

Ownership and intellectual property:

The ownership and intellectual property rights of the products or services developed or delivered through the alliance including any restrictions on their use and any obligations to protect confidential information.

Financial arrangements:

The financial arrangements between both partners including the allocation of costs and profits, the revenue sharing arrangements and the payment terms.

Dispute resolution:

The dispute resolution process for resolving any disputes that may arise between both partners including the use of mediation, arbitration, or litigation. This is such an important part of the agreement that it should be considered more than once and walked through by both parties together. More on this later in conflict resolution.

Termination:

The provisions for terminating the alliance including the circumstances under which the alliance may be terminated and the process for winding down the alliance.

It is important to work with legal counsel when drafting a strategic alliance contract to ensure that the contract complies with applicable laws and regulations and protects the interests of both partners.

CHAPTER SEVEN

ONBOARDING

Now that you've formed the alliance, it's time to onboard. Get this right and you're setting yourself, your teams, and the alliance up for success. Get it wrong, fail to manage expectations, fail to clearly define goals, objectives, and limitations, fail to define who does what, when, and why and you've set everyone up for a challenging alliance at best.

This is where mutual strategic planning really begins. The management of strategic alliances involves a healthy dose of strategic planning. It is the process of identifying and defining the alliance's goals, objectives and strategies. It involves creating a roadmap for the alliance and determining the steps needed to achieve the desired outcomes.

Develop a plan:

Develop a plan for onboarding the new alliance including the steps below and the timeline for each step.

Communicate the plan:

Communicate the plan to both parties and ensure everyone understands their roles and responsibilities.

Establish communication protocols:

Establish clear communication protocols between both parties including regular meetings and check-ins and a process for resolving disputes.

Train staff:

Provide training to all relevant staff members on the objectives and goals of the alliance and any new processes or procedures that may be required.

Share information:

Share all relevant information with the new alliance including any data or knowledge that may be useful in achieving their goals.

Commitments

Commitments are crucial to any strategic alliance as they help ensure that both partners work toward common goals and that the alliance succeeds. Contractual commitments mean both parties have skin in the game. Some key commitments that should be considered in a strategic alliance:

Shared goals and objectives:

Both partners should have a clear understanding of the goals and objectives of the alliance and should be committed to achieving these goals together. Clearly define the goals and objectives of the alliance.

Partners are more likely to be committed to the alliance if they have a clear understanding of what they are expected to achieve and why.

Investment of time and resources:

Both partners should be committed to investing the time and resources necessary to ensure the success of the alliance. This may include providing personnel, technology, or other resources.

Communication and collaboration:

Both partners should be committed to open and effective communication and collaboration. This will help to ensure that everyone is working toward a common goal and that information is shared effectively. Communicate regularly and openly. Regular and open communication can help build trust between partners and ensure that both partners are working toward common goals.

Performance expectations:

Both partners should have clear expectations for performance and should be committed to meeting these expectations. This may include meeting specific deadlines, delivering specific results, or maintaining certain quality standards.

Conflict resolution:

Both partners should be committed to resolving conflicts constructively and effectively and have a clear understanding of how conflicts will be addressed.

Continuous improvement:

Both partners should be committed to continuous improvement and work together to identify and implement opportunities for improvement.

Establish clear expectations and responsibilities:

Clearly defining expectations and responsibilities can help ensure everyone knows what is expected of them and is working toward the same goals.

Incentivize commitment: Consider offering incentives to partners who meet their commitments such as bonuses or special recognition.

Monitor progress:

Regularly monitoring progress can help to ensure that commitments are being met and can help to identify areas where additional support is needed.

Foster a culture of commitment:

Encourage partners to be committed to the alliance by fostering a culture that values and rewards commitment.

Define goals and objectives:

The first step is to clearly define the goals and objectives of the alliance. This involves clarifying what both partners hope to achieve through the alliance and establishing a shared understanding of what success looks like.

Allocate resources

Several types of resources can be utilized in a strategic allianced including:

Financial resources – including capital, funding, and financing options.

Human resources – including talent, expertise, and experience.

Technology resources – including software, hardware, and IT infrastructure.

Physical resources – including facilities, equipment, and supplies.

Intellectual property – including patents, trademarks, and copyrights.

Customer and market resources – including customer bases, market research, and data analysis.

Knowledge resources – including research and development, market trends, and industry insights.

Brand and marketing resources – including branding, marketing, and advertising resources and expertise.

The effective use of resources can help alliances achieve greater synergies and enhance their competitiveness, improving the chances of success.

Identify the objectives of the alliance:

Before defining processes it's important to understand the goals and objectives of the alliance. This will help you prioritize what processes need to be established and what is most important for the alliance to achieve.

Outline processes

As you would imagine, defining processes within strategic alliances are incredibly important in ensuring the success and sustainability of the partnership. These will be broadly based upon the industries the alliance operates within and the current processes and technologies used by both parties.

Determine the scope of the alliance:

Next, you need to determine the scope of the alliance. What functions will the alliance cover and what will each partner be responsible for? What is included in the alliance and what is excluded? Look at everything from marketing to sales to finance, support and everything in between.

Assign responsibilities:

Once the scope of the alliance is determined you can assign responsibilities to each partner. This will help ensure that each partner understands what they need to do and what is expected of them. Define these responsibilities clearly with as little ambiguity as possible. Think about managing expectations.

Develop a governance structure:

A governance structure is necessary for effective decision-making and ensuring all partners are aligned. This can, and should, include regular meetings, decision-making processes, and a process for conflict resolution.

Establish communication and reporting processes:

Communication, and managing expectations, is paramount to the success of any partnership. It's important to establish regular communication between partners as well as reporting processes to track progress and ensure that everyone is on the same page.

Define the metrics and KPIs:

To measure the alliance's success, it's important to define the metrics and KPIs that will be used. This could include revenue, market share, and customer satisfaction, among others. More on this later.

Review and refine processes:

Finally, it's important to review and refine the processes regularly to ensure they are still relevant and effective. Nothing is static in an alliance, if it is, you're treading water and likely close to drowning. Just as with any business, an alliance is constant process of refinement and sometimes pivoting.

Chapter Eight

People & Teams

Define roles and responsibilities:

The roles and responsibilities of each partner in the alliance should be clearly defined. This involves determining who will be responsible for specific tasks and activities and ensuring that everyone understands their role in the alliance.

Alliance Leaders

We defined what successful executive leaders and alliance managers look like earlier. Now it's time to select them.

Picking an executive leader for a strategic alliance requires careful consideration and due diligence. Here are the steps to follow:

Determine the skills and qualities needed:

Look at the type of strategic alliance and determine the skills and qualities needed in an executive leader. For example, a leader for a tech-focused alliance should have a strong understanding of the technologies in the space and its applications in addition to the customary executive leadership skills such a position requires.

Assess internal talent:

Evaluate the internal talent pool to see if anyone possesses the skills and qualities needed for the role.

Consider external candidates:

If no internal candidate is suitable, consider external candidates with the skills and experience required for the role.

Screen and interview:

Once you have a shortlist of candidates conduct thorough background checks and interviews to assess their suitability for the role.

Seek input from other stakeholders:

Consult with other stakeholders, such as key partners and customers, to gather their insights and opinions on the potential candidates.

Consider cultural fit:

Consider the cultural fit of the candidate as a misalignment in culture can cause problems in the long-term.

Make the final decision:

Based on the above factors make a final decision and appoint the executive leader for the strategic alliance.

The executive leader for a strategic alliance must have strong leadership skills, the ability to build and maintain relationships, excellent communication skills, and a deep understanding of the industry and market.

Extended teams

Extended teams in strategic alliances are groups of employees from partnering companies who work together to achieve specific goals or objectives within the alliance. These teams may consist of individuals with specific skill sets or expertise and are usually put together to address a specific business challenge or to take advantage of a specific opportunity. The extended team works together to leverage each other's strengths and resources to reach their objectives. This type of collaboration helps to increase the chances of success for the alliance and ensures that all partners are aligned and working together effectively.

Securing the buy-in of these members is perhaps the most important step. In many cases these extended team members work at an arms' distance from or work only occasionally within the alliance. For these team members to be effective they need to understand the mission, goals and objectives of the alliance, how it benefits the company and them indirectly, and the value they bring to the alliance.

Map relationships/org chart

Mapping relationships and creating org charts in strategic alliances is important because it helps to visualize and define the roles, responsibilities and communication channels within the partnership. This can help ensure that everyone involved clearly understands how they fit into the larger picture, what they are responsible for and who they need to communicate with. Having an org chart also helps to identify any potential gaps in the partnership and identify areas where resources may need to be reallocated to ensure success. It can also help to facilitate collaboration and coordination between partners and ensure that everyone is working toward the same goals. An org chart can also help organizations identify areas where they need to build or strengthen relationships and improve communication. All together, this can help create a more efficient and effective partnership and increase the likelihood of success.

Suggestions:

- Identify all key stakeholders involved in the alliance including employees, partners and customers.

- Determine and define the roles and responsibilities of each stakeholder and the relationships between them.

- Create a visual representation of the relationships and responsibilities using an org chart.

- Include information such as job titles, reporting lines and decision-making authority to help clarify the relationships and responsibilities.

- Regularly review and update the org chart to ensure it reflects the current state of the alliance.

- Use the org chart to help identify potential issues and opportunities in the alliance and to inform decision-making.

- Encourage open communication between stakeholders to help foster a strong alliance culture and keep everyone on the same page.

Secure buy-in

Securing buy-in from stakeholders is important in strategic alliances because it ensures that everyone is aligned and committed to the same goals and objectives. Without buy-in, there may be resistance or opposition to the alliance which can result in delays, confusion, and ultimately, failure. Buy-in helps to ensure that everyone is working together and that the alliance is moving in the right direction. Additionally, buy-in is crucial in gaining support for any necessary resources and decision-making processes which are essential to the alliance's success.

When securing buy-in for strategic alliances it is important to engage with key stakeholders from both organizations involved in the alliance. These stakeholders may be:

Executive leadership:

The CEO, President and other top executives who have the power to make decisions and set the direction of the organization.

Business unit leaders:

These leaders manage the specific business units that will be involved in the alliance and they have the expertise and knowledge to provide valuable insights into the alliance.

Operations and logistics:

The teams that are responsible for the day-to-day operations of the alliance including procurement, supply chain and logistics.

Finance and accounting:

The teams that manage the financial aspects of the alliance including budgeting, reporting and analysis.

Legal and contracts:

The teams responsible for reviewing and negotiating contracts and ensuring compliance with regulations and laws.

How to secure buy-in

Communicate the benefits:

Clearly articulate the benefits of the alliance to all stakeholders including partners, employees and customers.

Involve key stakeholders:

Make sure to involve key stakeholders in the decision-making process such as executive leaders, department heads and employees who will be directly impacted by the alliance.

Address concerns:

Address any concerns or objections that stakeholders may have. This could include issues related to business processes, data security, intellectual property or competition.

Develop a plan:

Develop a detailed plan that outlines the goals, responsibilities and expectations of each partner. Make sure the plan is clear, concise and easy to understand.

Build trust:

Build trust with your partners by being transparent, open and honest in your communication. Make sure that partners understand the benefits of the alliance and how it will impact their business.

Celebrate successes:

Celebrate successes along the way to reinforce the importance of the alliance and maintain buy-in from all stakeholders.

Monitor and adjust:

Continuously monitor the alliance to ensure that it is meeting the goals and expectations of all partners. Make adjustments as necessary to ensure the alliance continues to be successful.

CHAPTER NINE

FORMAL BUSINESS PLAN

Create a plan for how the alliance will work including decision-making processes, communication protocols, roles and responsibilities. It's important to think of an alliance as a business itself. A business within a business(es). Any successful business starts with a plan and an alliance is no different. And, virtually every part of a business plan for a stand-alone business will be part of strategic alliance business plan. The formal business plan should cover these key areas:

Define the purpose and goals of the alliance:

Clearly state what the alliance is designed to achieve and the specific objectives that will be met including the mission, objectives, vision, scope and strategy.

Identify the target market:

Determine the target market for the alliance and describe the benefits that the alliance will bring to the target market.

Develop a market analysis:

Perform a thorough market analysis to understand the size of the target market, market trends and competition.

Define the value proposition:

Clearly state what makes the alliance unique and how it will provide value to the target market.

Determine the resources required:

Identify the resources required to launch and run the alliance, including personnel, equipment and capital.

Develop a revenue model:

Identify the revenue sources for the alliance and determine how the revenue will be divided between the partners.

Define the operational structure:

Describe how the alliance will operate, including the roles and responsibilities of the partners, decision-making processes and communication channels.

Develop a risk management plan:

Identify potential risks to the alliance and develop a plan to mitigate those risks.

Develop a timeline:

Create a timeline that outlines the key milestones and deliverables for the alliance.

Present the plan:

Present the plan to key stakeholders, including the alliance partners and any other relevant parties, to secure buy-in and support.

Develop strategies:

Based on the market research, strategies can be developed to achieve the goals and objectives of the alliance. This involves identifying the resources that will be required, the activities that will be needed to be performed, and the steps that need to be taken to achieve the desired outcomes.

Go To Market Plan

The go-to-market plan can be part of the business plan or viewed as a stand-alone, supportive plan. Building a go-to-market plan for a strategic alliance requires careful planning, research and collaboration with your partner. Again, there are entire books written about go-to-market plans, start here:

Identify the target market:

Start by understanding who your target audience is and what their needs and wants are. This will help you determine the best way to reach them and what messaging will be most effective. This should be virtually readily available as both partner companies should already have identified their target markets. That is, unless the objective of the alliance is to target a new market.

Assess the market:

The next step is to assess the market and understand the competitive landscape. This involves researching the target market, analyzing the competition and identifying opportunities and challenges.

Define your offering:

Once you understand your target market you can develop your offering. In many cases your offering will be the same as it was previously although wrapped up in a new marketing and delivery system. If the offering is new, what products or services will you offer and how will you differentiate yourself from competitors?

Develop a messaging strategy:

Determine the key messages you want to communicate to your target audience and how you will communicate them. This will include your value proposition, positioning and branding. Presumably, one of the key objectives of the alliance is to deliver a new or improved value proposition by the partner companies partnering. Share that message.

Identify distribution channels:

Determine the best way to reach your target audience. This could include online marketing, direct sales, resellers or a combination of channels. These channels my be internal or may include new external means of distribution for one or both partners.

Determine sales and marketing resources:

Determine the resources that you will need to execute your go-to-market plan, including personnel, budgets and technology. It's often a good idea to put the marketing teams of both partner companies together with some alliance guidelines for them to do what they do best.

Establish key performance indicators (KPIs):

Define the KPIs/metrics that will be used to measure success, including revenue, market share, customer satisfaction and others. More on this elsewhere in the book.

Collaborate with your strategic alliance partner:

Work closely with your partner to ensure your go-to-market plan aligns with their goals and objectives. Ensure that you have clear communication and expectations regarding responsibilities and roles. Collaboration is key. In fact, a strategic alliance at its core is an intensive collaboration.

Continuously monitor and evaluate:

Continuously monitor the success of your go-to-market plan and make adjustments as needed. Regularly evaluate the performance of your KPIs and use the data to inform future decisions.

Financial model

Building a financial model for strategic alliances involves forecasting the expected financial outcomes of the partnership including revenue, expenses and profits. Building a financial model for a strategic alliance should include:

Define the goals and objectives of the strategic alliance:

Clearly outline the goals of the partnership and what each party expects to achieve. This will help guide the financial forecasting process.

Gather data:

Collect relevant financial data for each party such as historical financial statements, revenue projections and cost estimates.

Create revenue projections:

Based on the goals and data gathered, create projections for revenue that each partner can realistically expect to receive. This should be done for each product or service the strategic alliance offers.

Estimate costs:

Estimate the costs associated with the strategic alliance such as marketing, product development and administrative expenses.

Develop a profit and loss statement:

Combine the revenue projections and cost estimates to create a profit and loss statement. This will result in a detailed picture of the financial performance of the strategic alliance.

Cost to acquire:

Determining the cost to acquire in a strategic alliance involves considering the various expenses involved in forming the alliance such as negotiation costs, due diligence costs, legal fees and any upfront investments required. To determine the cost to acquire:

Identify the key expenses:

This includes all the costs involved in forming the alliance such as negotiations, legal fees, due diligence and up-front investments.

Estimate the cost of each expense:

Estimate the cost of each expense by researching the market rates for similar services and taking into account any specific requirements for the alliance.

Factor in the time frame:

The cost to acquire may vary depending on the time frame for forming the alliance so it's important to take this into consideration.

Calculate the total cost:

Add up all the estimated costs of the various expenses to determine the total cost to acquire.

Consider any contingencies:

It's always a good idea to factor in any contingencies, such as changes in market conditions, that may impact the cost to acquire.

Analyze the results:

Evaluate the financial model to see if it meets the goals and objectives of the strategic alliance. If not, revise the model and repeat the process until it is accurate and aligned with the goals of the partnership.

Regularly update the model:

It is important to regularly update the financial model as the strategic alliance evolves and new information becomes available. This will help ensure the partnership is on track to achieve its goals.

Sales Engagement plan

A sales engagement plan for a strategic alliance is important because it outlines the steps and actions that need to be taken to successfully sell the products or services offered through the alliance. This plan outlines the target market, the target customer segments and the sales channels to be used. It also includes the resources and budget required to support the sales effort. A sales engagement plan helps ensure everyone involved in the alliance is on the same page and working toward a common goal. This is especially important in strategic alliances where multiple organizations are involved and must work together effectively to achieve success.

A sales engagement plan for a strategic alliance should cover these areas:

Define the target market:

Identify the target customers and their needs that the alliance is trying to address.

Align sales goals and objectives:

Clearly define the sales goals and objectives of the alliance and how they align with both partners' goals.

Identify target customers:

Identify the key target customers that the alliance should target and their specific needs.

Develop a sales strategy:

Develop a sales strategy that takes into account the target market, target customers and the strengths of both partners.

Define sales processes and roles:

Define the sales process including how leads will be generated, how deals will be closed and who will be responsible for which activities.

Build a sales team:

Build a sales team with the right mix of skills, experience and commitment to achieve the sales goals of the alliance.

Develop sales enablement tools:

Develop sales enablement tools such as presentations, proposals and case studies, that the sales team can use to effectively engage with customers.

Train the sales team:

Provide training for the sales team to ensure they are equipped with the skills, knowledge and resources necessary to succeed. We dive further into this in Sales Enablement.

Monitor and evaluate performance:

Regularly monitor the sales team's performance and adjust the sales plan as necessary to ensure that the alliance's sales goals are being met.

Celebrate successes:

Celebrate the successes of the sales team and acknowledge their contributions to the success of the alliance.

Resource commitments

The resources that should be part of a strategic alliance can vary depending on the goals and objectives of the partnership but typically include these elements:

People:

A key part of any strategic alliance is the people involved including the executives and employees of each partner organization.

Financial resources:

Financial resources such as investment capital and budget are essential to support the partnership's initiatives and operations.

Technologies:

Technological resources such as software, hardware and data systems are often critical to the success of a strategic alliance.

Intellectual property:

Intellectual property like patents, trademarks and proprietary information are often valuable resources that can be leveraged in a strategic alliance.

Operations:

The operations of each partner including manufacturing, distribution and customer service can be integrated and optimized as part of a strategic alliance.

Marketing and sales:

Each partner's marketing and sales capabilities can be combined and leveraged to reach new customers and markets.

Data and analytics:

Data and analytics resources such as market research and customer insights are often critical to the success of a strategic alliance.

By pooling these resources partners can work together to achieve their goals and objectives more effectively and efficiently.

Exit strategy

An exit strategy for strategic alliances is a plan for ending the alliance which can be triggered by various circumstances such as changes in business goals, poor performance or changes in market conditions. Consider these:

Identify the potential reasons for ending the alliance:

Consider factors such as changes in market conditions, changes in business goals and poor performance of the alliance. It's a good idea to define some of the potential reasons ahead of time in the business plan or alliance agreement so that if there comes a time when there is a need to re-negotiate or exit, it comes as no surprise.

Define the terms of the exit:

Clearly outline the terms of the exit including the time frame, procedures and any financial or legal obligations.

Plan for the transition:

Consider how to manage the transition of responsibilities, resources and customer relationships during the exit. This should also be considered in the alliance agreement or business plan.

Consider alternative solutions:

Consider whether there are alternative solutions such as restructuring the alliance, finding a new partner or finding a different way to achieve the goals of the alliance.

Establish a communication plan:

Communicate the exit strategy to all relevant stakeholders including employees, customers and partners. Ensure that everyone understands the process and their role in it.

Continuously monitor and evaluate:

Continuously monitor the exit and evaluate whether the strategy needs to be modified to reflect changes in the business environment.

It is important to have an exit strategy in place to ensure that the alliance can be ended smoothly and efficiently, minimizing the impact on the business and stakeholders.

Playbook

A playbook for strategic alliances is a comprehensive document that outlines all the key processes, practices and procedures involved in managing and executing a strategic alliance. It acts as a roadmap for the alliance guiding both partners through all stages of the collaboration from initial planning to implementation and evaluation. A playbook should include a clear definition of the objectives and goals of the alliance as well as detailed information about the partner organizations, the structure of the alliance and the roles and responsibilities of each partner.

To create a playbook for strategic alliances, consider including this information and more:

Define the objectives and goals of the alliance:

Clearly articulate the goal of the alliance including specific targets and metrics to measure success.

Identify the partners involved in the alliance:

Outline the organizations that will be collaborating and their respective roles in the alliance.

Define the structure of the alliance:

Identify the key decision-making bodies, communication channels and processes for managing the alliance.

Define the roles and responsibilities of each partner:

Clearly articulate the responsibilities of each partner and ensure that these are aligned with the goals of the alliance.

Create a communication plan:

Outline the methods for communication between partners including regular meetings, reports and regular feedback mechanisms.

Establish a decision-making process:

Establish a clear and transparent process for making decisions and resolving conflicts that may arise during the course of the alliance.

Define the processes for monitoring and evaluating the alliance:

Establish clear processes for monitoring progress, evaluating results and making any necessary adjustments to the alliance as it evolves.

A playbook should provide a clear and comprehensive guide to managing a strategic alliance, ensuring that both partners are on the same page and that the alliance is executed effectively.

CHAPTER TEN

OPERATE

Sales Enablement

Sales enablement refers to the strategies, processes and tools used to help sales teams be more effective and efficient in their selling activities. The goal of sales enablement is to improve the sales process from lead generation to closing deals by providing salespeople with the information and resources they need to sell more effectively. In other words, improving their capabilities. Improving partner capabilities in a strategic alliance is vital to its long-term success and perhaps the most valuable action in enabling your alliance partners to be successful. Here are some ways to improve partner capabilities:

Provide training and development opportunities:

Provide training and development opportunities for your partners including training programs, webinars, printed materials, workshops and conferences. It important to help your partners to develop the skills and knowledge they need to succeed for the success of the alliance.

Sales training:

Providing sales teams with training on the products and services they sell, as well as on sales techniques and best practices. The better your partner sells, the better the alliances chance of success.

Sales enablement technology:

Providing sales teams with tools and technology such as customer relationship management (CRM) systems and marketing automation platforms to help them sell more effectively.

Sales content:

Providing sales teams with the content they need to sell such as product brochures, presentations, pricing and case studies.

Sales coaching and support:

Providing sales teams with coaching and support such as regular check-ins, performance evaluations and mentoring programs is an often expected benefit of an alliance.

The goal of sales enablement is to empower sales teams to be more effective and efficient in their selling activities, ultimately leading to increased sales and revenue for the company.

Production goals

Production goals are specific, measurable targets that are set for the production of goods or services. These goals can be related to the production of a particular product, line of products or the entire company's production output.

Some common production goals:

Quantity goals: Targets for the number of units of a particular product or service that will be produced during a specified period.

Quality goals: Targets for the quality standards that must be met for a particular product or service.

Efficiency goals: Targets for the amount of time or resources it takes to produce a particular product or service.

Setting production goals in a strategic alliance:

Setting sales production goals in a strategic alliance requires a collaborative effort between the partners. Consider these when setting goals:

Assess the market:

Analyze the market and the target customer segment to determine the potential for sales and revenue. This will help in setting realistic and achievable sales goals.

Define objectives:

Establish clear, measurable objectives for the strategic alliance, focusing on specific targets for sales and revenue growth.

Allocate responsibilities:

Assign specific roles and responsibilities for the sales and marketing efforts ensuring that each partner is clear on what they are responsible for.

Establish metrics:

Establish metrics for measuring progress and success such as the number of leads generated, the conversion rate and the revenue generated. More on metrics later.

Develop a sales plan:

Work together to develop a detailed sales plan outlining the steps that will be taken to achieve the sales goals including marketing and sales initiatives, strategies, target markets, tools and sales processes.

Review and adjust:

Regularly review the production goals as needed. This can be done annually or sometimes more often depending upon the success or failure to reach the current goals.

Share best practices:

Share best practices and knowledge with your partners. This can help them improve their processes and operations and better meet their customers' needs.

Encourage collaboration:

Encourage collaboration between your partners and your own organization. This can help build trust, foster a positive relationship, improve processes and provide opportunities for both parties to learn from each other.

Offer support:

Offer support to your partners in areas where they may need assistance. This could include providing resources, mentorship, technical support, customer support or advice.

Provide access to resources:

Provide access to resources such as technology, data, tools, teams, training and financial commitments to help your partners improve their capabilities.

Foster a culture of continuous improvement:

Foster a culture of continuous improvement within the alliance encouraging both partners to continuously seek out new opportunities for growth and development.

CHAPTER ELEVEN

COMMUNICATION

Define communication channels:

Knowing how and who to communicate with is a fundamental function of getting strategic alliances right. Everyone working within the alliance should have clear understanding of what to communicate, to whom, when and how. This will eliminate a lot of potential busy work and friction.

Foster open communication:

Regular communication is critical to the success of a strategic alliance. Encourage open, honest, regular and transparent communication between both parties.

Foster trust:

Foster trust between both parties by honoring commitments, being transparent and open in communication and recognizing the value of each other's contributions. Fostering trust in strategic alliances is crucial for their success. Here are some suggestions to help foster trust:

Communicate openly:

Encourage open and honest communication between both parties. This helps build trust by reducing misunderstandings and keeping everyone on the same page.

Honoring commitments:

Make sure to follow through on all commitments whether big or small. This builds trust by showing that you are reliable and can be counted on.

Sharing information:

Share relevant information with your alliance partner even if it is sensitive or potentially damaging. This shows that you trust them and are willing to be transparent.

Being transparent:

Be open and transparent in your dealings with your alliance partner. This includes being upfront about any challenges or obstacles that may arise.

Recognizing each other's contributions:

Acknowledge and appreciate the contributions of each party. This helps build trust by showing that you value and respect each other.

Building a personal relationship:

Building a personal relationship with your alliance partner can also help foster trust. This can be achieved through regular communication, socializing and finding common interests.

Creating a shared culture:

Creating a shared culture between both parties can help foster trust by encouraging collaboration and a sense of teamwork.

Maintaining ethical behavior:

Maintaining ethical behavior and adhering to the agreed-upon rules and guidelines is crucial for building trust in a strategic alliance. This helps to ensure that both parties are acting in good faith and with the best interests of the alliance in mind.

CHAPTER TWELVE

<u>MARKETING</u>

Co-marketing is an effective way to promote both partners' brands and products in a strategic alliance. Here are some steps to succeed at co-marketing in a strategic alliance:

Define goals and objectives:

Define the goals and objectives for the co-marketing efforts including the target audience, messaging, delivery methods and desired outcomes.

Develop a co-marketing plan:

Develop a co-marketing plan that outlines the tactics and strategies for executing the co-marketing efforts. This could include social media campaigns, email marketing, joint events, webinars, conferences and more.

Collaborate on messaging:

Collaborate with your partner on messaging and branding to ensure that the co-marketing efforts align with both partners' brand values and messaging guidelines.

Allocate resources:

Allocate resources such as time, budget and personnel to support the co-marketing efforts. This may include staff time, marketing materials, conference spend, travel and other resources.

Track and measure results:

Track and measure the results of the co-marketing efforts using metrics such as website traffic, social media engagement, requests for information, follow-up actions from the sale and marketing teams, lead/opportunity generation and sales.

Continuously evaluate and improve:

Continuously evaluate and improve the co-marketing efforts based on the results and feedback from both partners to help ensure the efforts are effective and are aligned with the goals and objectives of the strategic alliance.

Foster a culture of collaboration:

Foster a culture of collaboration and communication between both partners to ensure that the co-marketing efforts are aligned and effective. This may include scheduling team meetings or outings or benchmarking best practices between teams.

CHAPTER THIRTEEN

TECHNOLOGY

Technology plays a crucial role in strategic alliances as it helps to streamline processes, increase efficiency, deliver results and enhance communication between partners. This includes using technology to:

Collaborate on projects and initiatives:

Collaboration tools such as project management software, virtual whiteboards, sales tools like CRM's and document-sharing platforms help to streamline collaboration between partners.

Monitor performance:

Technology such as monitoring and reporting tools can help track the alliance's performance, identify areas for improvement and hold partners accountable.

Enhance communication:

Communication technologies such as instant messaging, video conferencing and webinars help to enhance communication and foster closer relationships between partners.

Improve data security:

Strategic alliances often involve sharing sensitive information and data which requires the use of secure data storage and transfer technologies to protect against potential breaches.

Streamline processes:

Automated systems can help to streamline processes such as data tracking, invoicing, opportunity sharing and reporting, reducing manual workloads and freeing up time for strategic activities.

Technology sharing:

Shared technology in strategic alliances refers to the use of technology by two or more companies that have formed a strategic alliance. The goal of shared technology is to leverage each company's expertise, resources, and technological capabilities to achieve common business objectives. This can involve sharing software, hardware, data, or other forms of technology. Shared technology is often used to streamline processes, improve product development and delivery and increase the overall efficiency of the strategic alliance. Some common examples of shared technology in strategic alliances include cloud computing, data analytics, and artificial intelligence. By sharing technology, strategic alliances can reduce costs, increase speed to market and create new business opportunities.

CHAPTER FOURTEEN

SERVICE & SUPPORT

Service and support are critical components of a successful strategic alliance. The objective of service and support is to ensure that customers are receiving the best possible service and support from both partners in the alliance. This includes ensuring that customers have access to the right expertise, support and training to make the most of the products and services offered.. The service and support team should understand the customers' needs, the products and services offered and how they support the overall goals of the strategic alliance. The service and support function should be well integrated into the overall strategic alliance process ensuring that customers receive consistent and effective support.

Some important steps to building a strong service and support framework in a strategic alliance:

Define roles and responsibilities:

Clearly outline the roles and responsibilities of each partner in providing service and support to customers. This helps to avoid misunderstandings and ensures that customers receive the necessary support in a timely manner.

Establish protocols for communication and escalation:

Ensure that there are clear protocols for communication and escalation in case of any issues or challenges. It's also important to facilitate open lines of communication between support teams along with clearly defined processes for each team to manage to expectations. This helps to resolve problems quickly and effectively.

Build a strong support team:

Build a strong support team with individuals who are knowledgeable and skilled in the products and services being offered. This team should be able to provide excellent customer service and support.

Utilize technology:

Utilize technology such as customer relationship management (CRM) systems and remote support tools, to manage and track support requests, cases, and resolutions.

Regularly review and improve processes:

Regularly review and improve processes to ensure that they are efficient and effective. This helps to identify any areas for improvement and make necessary changes.

Provide training and development opportunities:

Provide training and development opportunities to support team members to help them keep their skills and knowledge up-to-date and provide excellent customer service and support.

CHAPTER FIFTEEN

REVENUE

Revenue is an important consideration in any strategic alliance as it is often one of the primary goals of the partnership. There are many ways to generate revenue in strategic alliances, including:

Joint product development:

Partners can work together to develop and market new products sharing the revenue generated from sales.

Cross-selling:

Partners can work together to cross-sell each other's products or services generating new revenue streams for both partners.

Joint marketing:

Partners can collaborate on joint marketing efforts such as co-branded advertising or promotions to increase awareness and sales.

Joint ventures:

Partners can form a joint venture with each partner contributing resources and expertise and sharing in the profits generated from the venture.

Licensing:

One partner can license its products or technologies to the other generating revenue through licensing fees.

Cost sharing:

Partners can work together to reduce costs by sharing resources or pooling purchasing power and sharing the savings generated.

It is important to have clear agreements in place that outline how revenue will be generated and shared between partners. This will help to ensure that both partners are aligned on the goals of the alliance and to eliminate misunderstandings.

CHAPTER SIXTEEN

MANAGING FINANCES

Managing finances in strategic alliances is important for evaluating their long-term success. Let's face it; financial success is the ultimate goal:

Define financial goals and objectives:

Define the financial goals and objectives for the alliance including budget, revenue targets, cost to acquire and cost-saving initiatives.

Develop a budget:

Develop a budget for the alliance taking into account the financial goals and objectives as well as the resources and personnel needed to achieve these goals.

Agree on financial management processes:

Agree on the financial management processes for the alliance including the reporting and reconciliation procedures as well as the processes and people involved in managing risk and uncertainty.

Track and monitor financial performance:

Track and monitor the financial performance of the alliance using metrics such as revenue growth, profitability, cost to acquire, margins and return on investment.

Communicate financial information:

Communicate financial information to both partners regularly to ensure that both partners have a clear understanding of the financial performance of the alliance.

Review and adjust financial plans:

Review and adjust financial plans regularly to ensure that the financial goals and objectives of the alliance remain aligned with the overall goals and objectives of the alliance.

Foster transparency and trust:

Foster transparency and trust between both partners to ensure that financial information is shared openly and honestly and that both partners have confidence in the financial management.

Chapter Seventeen

Measure

Regular monitoring and tracking of progress are important to ensure that the alliance performs. This includes evaluating the performance of the alliance to ensure it is meeting the goals and objectives set out in the agreement. If the alliance is not working, make necessary changes to improve it or consider terminating the relationship.

Tracking strategic alliances:

Periodic reviews of strategic alliances are an important aspect of managing these relationships and ensuring their continued success. Reviews may be performed as often as weekly in the early stages. Here are some steps to help you conduct effective strategic alliance reviews:

Schedule the review:

Schedule the review at a regular interval such as once a quarter or once a year and give adequate notice to the alliance partner so that they can prepare for the review.

Define the goals and objectives:

Define the goals and objectives of the review including what areas will be covered and what information will be gathered.

Gather data:

Gather data from various sources, including internal stakeholders, alliance partners, and market research, to help you assess the performance of the alliance. It's a good idea to share the data with the partner ahead of the performance review so that the partner has time to digest the data in comparison with their data and have time to formulate questions and potential follow-up actions for discussion.

Evaluate performance:

Evaluate the performance of the alliance against the agreed-upon goals and objectives and assess whether the alliance is delivering the expected results.

To evaluate performance the data must be measured. Here are some HPIs/metrics that can be used to measure the success of a strategic alliance:

Financial performance:

Financial metrics such as revenue growth, profitability, cost to acquire and return on investment can be used to measure the financial success of the alliance.

Market share:

Market share is a measure of how much of the market a company or alliance has captured. Measuring market share can help to assess the competitive position of the alliance.

Customer satisfaction:

Customer satisfaction can be measured by surveying customers or by tracking customer feedback and complaints. High levels of customer satisfaction indicate that the alliance is delivering value to its customers.

Operational efficiency:

Operational efficiency can be measured by tracking key performance indicators such as delivery time, production costs, allocated team member time and process cycle time. Improving operational efficiency can help to reduce costs and increase productivity.

Employee satisfaction:

Employee satisfaction can be measured by surveying employees or by tracking employee engagement and turnover. High levels of employee satisfaction indicate that the alliance is creating a positive work environment.

Innovation:

Innovation can be measured by tracking the number of new products, services or processes the alliance has introduced. A high rate of innovation indicates that the alliance is adapting to changing market conditions and is well-positioned for future success.

Market recognition:

Market recognition can be measured by tracking media coverage, awards, customer comments / testimonials and other forms of recognition. High levels of market recognition indicate that the alliance is well-regarded in its industry.

Strategic alignment:

Strategic alignment can be measured by tracking the degree to which the goals and objectives of both parties are aligned. A high degree of alignment indicates that the alliance is functioning effectively and is well-positioned to achieve its goals.

CHAPTER EIGHTEEN

METRICS & KPIS

Measuring the success of a strategic alliance is critical to ensuring it meets its goals and objectives. Metrics and KPIs (Key Performance Indicators) can be used to track the performance of a strategic alliance and identify areas for improvement.

KPI (Key Performance Indicator) and metrics are two terms often used interchangeably, but they are slightly different in meaning.

Metrics are often quantitative measures of performance. They are data-driven and provide a snapshot of an organization's performance at a specific point in time. Examples of metrics include revenue, profit, customer satisfaction and time to market.

On the other hand, KPI is often a subset of metrics considered critical to an organization's success. They are chosen to align with the organization's goals and objectives and are used to track the performance of specific areas of the business. KPIs are often used to track the performance of a particular project or initiative such as a strategic alliance.

Some common metrics and KPIs for strategic alliances:

Revenue growth:

The growth in revenue generated by the strategic alliance includes both the revenue generated by new products or services and the revenue growth generated by existing products or services.

Market share:

The market share of the products or services developed or delivered through the strategic alliance compared to the market share of similar products or services offered by competitors.

Cost savings:

The cost savings generated by the strategic alliance including the savings generated by shared resources, joint procurement and other cost-saving initiatives often measured in cost to acquire.

Customer satisfaction:

The level of customer satisfaction with the products or services developed or delivered through the strategic alliance as measured through customer feedback and surveys or public comments.

Partner satisfaction:

The level of satisfaction of both partners with the strategic alliance as measured through regular partner surveys and feedback.

Time to market:

The time to market for new products or services developed or delivered through the strategic alliance compared to the time to market for similar products or services offered by competitors.

Market penetration:

The penetration of the target market by the products or services developed or delivered through the strategic alliance as measured by the number of customers and the size of the market.

Return on investment:

The return on investment for both partners as measured by the financial performance of the strategic alliance and the financial benefits generated by the alliance.

By regularly monitoring and analyzing these metrics and KPIs, organizations can ensure that their strategic alliance performs effectively and delivers value to both partners.

CHAPTER NINETEEN

REVIEWS

Strategic alliance reviews are regular assessments of the performance and effectiveness of a strategic alliance. They are an important tool for ensuring that the alliance is meeting its goals and objectives and for identifying areas for improvement. Key elements of a strategic alliance review:

Goals and objectives:

A review of the goals and objectives of the alliance including a comparison of the current performance of the alliance to the goals and objectives set at the start of the alliance.

Financial performance:

A review of the financial performance of the alliance including the revenue generated by the alliance, the cost savings generated by the alliance, the cost to acquire new customers and sell products & services and the return on investment for both partners.

Market performance:

A review of the market performance of the alliance including the market share of the products or services developed or delivered through the alliance, the customer satisfaction with the products or services and the market penetration of the target market.

Partner satisfaction:

A review of the satisfaction of both partners with the alliance including a review of the communication and collaboration between the partners and the level of trust and commitment between the partners.

Performance of key initiatives:

A review of the performance of key initiatives and projects within the alliance including a review of the time to market for new products or services, customer satisfaction, innovation, and the performance of any co-marketing initiatives.

Recommendations for improvement:

A review of any areas for improvement in the alliance and recommendations for addressing any challenges or obstacles facing the alliance.

Address any issues:

Address any issues that have arisen during the alliance and determine how they can be resolved or prevented in the future.

Agree on an action plan:

Agree on an action plan with the alliance partner which should include specific steps to improve the alliance and address any areas of concern.

Document the review:

Document the review and its outcome, including any agreed-upon action items, so that they can be tracked and implemented over time.

Address any challenges:

If any challenges arise address them promptly and work to find a solution that benefits both parties. This is referred to as conflict resolution.

Regular strategic alliance reviews are critical to the success of a strategic alliance, as they provide an opportunity to assess the performance of the alliance, identify areas for improvement and make changes to ensure that the alliance is meeting its goals and objectives.

CHAPTER TWENTY

CONFLICT RESOLUTION

Conflict resolution or dispute resolution is an often overlooked yet critically important aspect of managing strategic alliances. Dispute resolution in strategic alliances refers to the process of resolving conflicts that may arise between partners in a strategic alliance. This can include disagreements over business objectives, management responsibilities, or revenue sharing among other things. Dispute resolution processes are typically established ahead of time and agreed upon by both partners in the strategic alliance agreement. Dispute resolution in strategic alliances is crucial because conflicts and disagreements can (and will) arise between partners during the alliance. These conflicts can arise for various reasons such as different business objectives, conflicting goals, misaligned expectations and misinterpreting agreements. Dispute resolution is important to resolve these conflicts efficiently and effectively and to prevent the alliance from falling apart or causing significant damage to the partners. A well-designed dispute resolution process can help to mitigate the risk of disputes and to maintain the integrity of the alliance. Again, it's about managing expectations rather than fixing misunderstandings.

Identify the conflict:

The first step in resolving conflict is to identify the cause of the conflict. This may involve talking to both parties and gathering information to understand the issue.

Establish a communication channel:

Communication is the first step in resolving disputes is to have open and honest communication between both partners. Both partners must clearly express their concerns and discuss the issue. Establish a clear and open communication channel between both parties to allow for a constructive dialogue.

Agree on a common goal:

Agree on a common goal for resolving the conflict. This helps ensure that both parties work toward a mutually acceptable outcome.

Identify the underlying issues:

Identify the underlying issues that are contributing to the conflict. This may involve exploring both parties' perspectives and understanding the motivations behind their actions.

Brainstorm solutions:

Brainstorm potential solutions to the conflict. This may involve seeking input from both parties and considering a range of options.

Mediation:

If the issue cannot be resolved through communication it is recommended to involve a neutral third-party mediator who can facilitate a resolution.

Contractual Agreements:

Having a clear and comprehensive contract in place can help avoid disputes in the first place. The contract should include a dispute resolution clause that outlines the process to be followed in case of a dispute.

Collaboration:

The parties involved in the dispute should work together to find a mutually acceptable solution. Collaboration helps to keep the partnership intact and ensures that the issue is resolved to the satisfaction of both parties.

Legal Action:

Legal action may be taken as a last resort if all other methods have failed. However, this should be avoided as it can be costly and time-consuming and may have a negative impact on the partnership.

Agree on a resolution:

Agree on a resolution that meets the needs of both parties. This may involve compromising, negotiating or finding a mutually acceptable solution.

Implement the solution:

Implement the agreed-upon solution and monitor the situation to ensure that the conflict has been resolved.

Follow-up:

Follow-up with both parties to ensure that the solution has been effective and to prevent similar conflicts from arising in the future.

Foster trust:

Foster trust between both parties by encouraging open and honest communication, recognizing each other's contributions and working together to resolve any challenges that may arise.

Celebrate successes:

Celebrate the successes of the alliance and acknowledge the contributions of both parties.

Review and renew:

Regularly review the alliance and assess whether it is still meeting the objectives. Consider renewing or terminating the alliance if necessary.

Strategic planning is an ongoing process that requires continuous review and adjustment to ensure that the alliance remains aligned with the changing needs of the market and the partners. It is important to have a clear and effective dispute resolution process in place to ensure that disputes are resolved quickly and efficiently and to prevent damage to the strategic alliance.

CHAPTER TWENTY-ONE

<u>ADAPT</u>

There are several reasons why a strategic alliance may need to pivot or change. Some of the reasons may be:

Market changes:

The market environment may change and impact the viability of the alliance. The alliance may need to pivot to stay relevant in the changing market.

Partner changes:

The partner company may change its strategy or goals which can affect the alliance. The alliance may need to be adapted to accommodate the changes in the partner company.

Performance issues:

The alliance may not be delivering the desired results and may need to be changed to improve its performance.

Unforeseen challenges:

The alliance may face unforeseen challenges that may require changes to the agreement.

New opportunities:

The alliance may uncover new opportunities that may require changes to the agreement to take advantage of them.

To adapt strategic alliances, try these:

Assess the current state of the alliance:

Evaluate the current status of the alliance including the goals, objectives and performance.

Identify areas for improvement:

Look for areas where the alliance could be improved and focus on specific areas where performance could be enhanced.

Communicate changes:

Communicate the changes to the alliance partners and discuss how the changes will benefit the partnership.

Agree on new goals:

Identify new goals for the alliance and agree on specific targets for each partner.

Update processes and systems:

Make changes to the processes and systems that support the alliance to ensure they are aligned with the new goals.

Review and monitor progress:

Regularly review and monitor progress to ensure the changes are being implemented and the alliance is on track.

Foster open communication:

Foster open communication between the partners to ensure they are aligned and working toward the same goals.

Continuously evaluate:

Continuously evaluate the alliance and make changes as necessary to ensure it remains effective and aligned with business objectives.

Chapter Twenty-Two

What to Expect Out of Alliances

The results of strategic alliances for companies or businesses can vary depending on the objectives and goals of the alliance. However, here are some common outcomes and benefits of strategic alliances:

Increased market presence:

Strategic alliances can help companies increase their market presence by expanding their reach and accessing new customers.

Improved competitiveness:

Alliances can help companies become more competitive by leveraging the strengths and resources of their partners.

Shared risk and cost:

Strategic alliances can help companies share the risk and costs associated with developing new products or entering new markets.

Improved access to technology and knowledge:

Alliances can provide companies access to new technologies and knowledge they may not have had otherwise.

Improved product offerings:

Alliances can result in the development of new and improved products that can be offered to customers.

Increased revenue and profitability:

By expanding their reach, improving competitiveness and developing new products, strategic alliances can help companies increase their revenue and profitability.

Strategic alliances can provide companies with a wide range of benefits and outcomes including increased market presence, improved competitiveness, shared risk and cost, improved access to technology and knowledge, improved product offerings, and increased revenue and profitability.

CHAPTER TWENTY-THREE

EXAMPLES

Several companies have a reputation for being successful in strategic alliances, including:

Procter & Gamble:

This consumer goods company has a history of successful strategic alliances with a range of partners including partnerships with Walmart, Amazon and Johnson & Johnson.

Boeing:

The aerospace giant has a history of successful strategic alliances including partnerships with Airbus and General Electric.

Amazon:

Amazon has been successful in strategic alliances with a range of partners including collaborations with companies such as Whole Foods, UPS and FedEx.

Microsoft:

Microsoft has a history of successful strategic alliances including partnerships with Dell, HP and Intel.

Pfizer:

Pfizer has a reputation for being successful in strategic alliances with partnerships with companies such as Merck, GlaxoSmithKline and Sanofi.

Coca-Cola:

Coca-Cola has a history of successful strategic alliances including collaborations with companies such as McDonald's, PepsiCo and Nestle.

Toyota:

Toyota has a reputation for being successful in strategic alliances with partnerships with companies such as General Motors, BMW and Ford.

These companies have established a strong track record of successful strategic alliances through careful planning, effective management and a focus on shared goals and objectives.

CHAPTER TWENTY-FOUR

STRATEGIC ALLIANCE CASE STUDIES

Strategic alliance case studies are studies of real-life partnerships between companies that have formed strategic alliances to achieve common goals. These case studies provide valuable insights into the various aspects of strategic alliances including the motivations behind forming such alliances, the process of finding and selecting partners, the challenges that arise during the alliance and the results achieved. Some popular strategic alliance case studies include the alliance between Starbucks and PepsiCo, the alliance between Apple and AT&T and the alliance between Nike and Adidas. These case studies can be used to learn best practices and lessons in forming, managing and measuring the success of strategic alliances. They can be found in academic journals, business publications and online resources.

Chapter Twenty-Five

Successes

Coke and Pepsi:

The first example of a successful strategic alliance case study is the partnership between Coca-Cola and PepsiCo. In the 1990s, these two competitors came together to create a strategic alliance for producing and distributing fountain drinks in restaurants and fast food chains. The goal was to increase efficiency and reduce costs for both companies.

Through this alliance, both companies were able to benefit from shared distribution systems and marketing campaigns. As a result, they were able to reach a wider customer base and increase sales. In addition, they were able to reduce costs by pooling resources and sharing the burden of investment in new technology and equipment.

This strategic alliance has been successful for both companies and they have continued to work together to this day. The partnership has allowed both companies to remain competitive in the market and to continue to grow and expand.

Apple and IBM:

Another example of a successful strategic alliance is the partnership between Apple and IBM in 2014. This partnership aimed to create and deliver enterprise solutions for iOS devices. IBM provided its industry-leading enterprise expertise, software and services, while Apple provided its hardware and iOS platform. This partnership was successful in delivering industry-specific enterprise solutions, such as those for the banking, retail and insurance sectors. The collaboration between these two tech giants resulted in a range of enterprise solutions that helped to increase productivity, cost-effectiveness and efficiency for their clients. This alliance is widely regarded as a win-win for both companies and demonstrates the power of strategic alliances in driving business growth and innovation.

Apple and AT&T:

Another case study is the partnership between Apple and AT&T. In 2007, Apple launched the iPhone and AT&T became its exclusive carrier in the US. This strategic alliance helped both companies achieve their goals. Apple was able to expand its market reach and AT&T increased its customer base, propelling AT&T to become the leading mobile carrier in the United States. The partnership was beneficial for both companies as it allowed them to access new customers and revenue streams. This strategic alliance helped AT&T establish itself as a leader in the mobile phone market and Apple solidified its position as a market innovator and established a dominant position in the smartphone market. This partnership was a classic example of two companies coming together to achieve a shared goal and it helped both companies grow and succeed in their respective markets.

Boeing and Airbus:

In 1987, Boeing and Airbus formed a strategic alliance to jointly develop the next-generation air traffic control system. The alliance was a success as it allowed both companies to share the cost of development and increase their competitiveness in the market.

Nike and Adidas:

In 2006, Nike and Adidas formed a strategic alliance to jointly develop sustainable technologies and materials for their athletic footwear and clothing products. This alliance was successful as it allowed both companies to share the cost of research and development and improve their sustainability efforts.

Toyota and Tesla:

In 2010, Toyota and Tesla formed a strategic alliance to jointly develop electric vehicles and battery technology. This alliance was successful as it allowed both companies to share the cost of research and development and improve their competitiveness in the electric vehicle market.

These success stories demonstrate the potential of strategic alliances to help companies expand their market reach, leverage strengths and resources, share risk and cost, access new technologies and knowledge, increase revenue and profitability and strengthen brand image and reputation.

CHAPTER TWENTY-SIX

<u>FAILURES</u>

Daimler-Chrysler:

In 1998, Daimler-Benz merged with Chrysler to form Daimler-Chrysler, a global automotive alliance. However, the alliance was unsuccessful as both companies struggled to align their corporate cultures, visions and strategies. As a result, Daimler-Chrysler faced declining sales, high costs, low employee morale and weak brand image. The alliance ultimately failed, as Daimler sold Chrysler in 2007.

Yahoo and Google:

In 2000, Yahoo and Google formed a strategic alliance to develop and distribute search and advertising services. However, the alliance was not successful as both companies faced intense competition from other search engines and online advertising platforms. As a result, Yahoo and Google faced declining market share, low revenue growth and weak brand image. The alliance ultimately failed as Yahoo chose to end the partnership and develop its own search and advertising services.

Sears and Kmart:

In 2005, Sears and Kmart formed a strategic alliance to jointly develop and operate a new chain of discount department stores. However, the alliance was unsuccessful as both companies faced intense competition from other discount retailers and operational challenges, such as supply chain management, store quality and customer service. As a result, Sears and Kmart faced declining sales, low customer satisfaction, and weak brand image. The alliance ultimately failed, and Sears and Kmart faced bankruptcy and the closure of many stores.

HP and Compaq:

In 2001, HP and Compaq merged to form a global technology alliance. However, the alliance was not successful as both companies faced intense competition from other technology companies and struggled to align their corporate cultures, visions and strategies. As a result, HP and Compaq faced declining sales, high costs, low employee morale and weak brand image. The alliance ultimately failed.

These failure stories demonstrate the risks and challenges of strategic alliances such as cultural differences, competition, operational difficulties, cost, quality and image issues. Companies must carefully evaluate and manage these factors to ensure the success of their strategic alliances and avoid costly and damaging failures.

CHAPTER TWENTY-SEVEN

SUCCESS RATES

The success rate of strategic alliances can vary depending on many factors such as the industry, the type of alliance and the level of preparation and collaboration between the partners. However, here are some statistics on the success of strategic alliances:

50% success rate:

According to a survey by the Harvard Business Review, 50% of strategic alliances succeed and deliver the expected results.

75% success rate:

Another study by Accenture found that 75% of strategic alliances are successful in achieving their objectives.

Short-term vs. long-term success:

A report by McKinsey found that short-term strategic alliances have a higher success rate of 70-80%, while long-term alliances have a success rate of 60-70%.

Industry-specific success:

The success rate of strategic alliances can vary depending on the industry. For example, alliances in the technology industry have a higher success rate of around 80%, while alliances in the pharmaceutical industry have a lower success rate of around 50%.

These statistics suggest that while the success rate of strategic alliances can vary, there is a general understanding that around 50-75% of strategic alliances are successful in achieving their objectives. However, it is important to note that the success of an alliance depends on several factors such as the preparation and collaboration of the partners and the ability to effectively manage the alliance over time.

CHAPTER TWENTY-EIGHT

<u>TOOLS</u>

Many tools can be used to manage strategic alliances, including:

Project Management Tools:

Project management tools such as Asana, Trello, or Basecamp can help you track progress and keep everyone in the alliance on the same page.

Collaboration Tools:

Tools like Slack, Microsoft Teams, or Google Workspace can help teams communicate and collaborate more effectively.

Performance Metrics Tools:

Tools like KPIs and dashboards can help you monitor the performance of the alliance and make data-driven decisions.

Contract Management Tools:

Tools like DocuSign, Adobe Sign, or Proposify can help you manage contracts and keep track of deadlines and milestones.

Business Intelligence Tools:

Tools like Tableau, Power BI, or QlikView can help you analyze data and understand trends in the alliance.

CRM Tools:

CRM tools like Salesforce or HubSpot can help you manage relationships with customers and partners in the alliance.

Scorecard:

A strategic alliance scorecard is a tool used to measure and monitor the performance of a strategic alliance. It provides a systematic way of evaluating the alliance's success by tracking key performance indicators (KPIs) such as revenue, costs, market share, customer satisfaction and other relevant metrics. The scorecard helps to identify areas for improvement and provides a basis for making decisions about the future direction of the alliance. By regularly monitoring the alliance with a scorecard, partners can ensure that the alliance is on track to meet its goals and make necessary adjustments as needed.

Give to Get:

A give-to-get tracking tool is a tool used to measure the mutual benefits and returns of a strategic alliance. It helps keep track of the commitments and contributions made by each partner in the alliance and ensures that both partners benefit equally from the relationship. This tool helps evaluate the alliance's success, identify any imbalances and make necessary adjustments to ensure that both partners are receiving the expected benefits. By tracking the give-and-get in the alliance both partners can be confident that the alliance is moving in the right direction and that both partners are benefiting from the relationship.

These tools can help streamline the management process and make it easier to monitor and track the success of the alliance.

CHAPTER TWENTY-NINE

STRATEGIC ALLIANCE MANAGER JOB DESCRIPTION

A Strategic Alliance Manager is responsible for identifying and establishing strategic partnerships with other companies or organizations that can benefit their own organization. This includes identifying potential partners, negotiating partnerships, and managing the relationships to ensure they meet both organizations' goals and objectives. The job duties of a Strategic Alliance Manager may include:

- Identifying potential strategic partners and evaluating their suitability.

- Negotiating terms and conditions of partnerships, including joint ventures, co-marketing agreements, and other types of alliances.

- Developing and implementing strategies to grow and maintain the partnerships.

- Coordinating cross-functional teams to execute alliance initiatives.

- Communicating regularly with partners to understand their needs and goals and ensure the partnership meets their expectations.

- Assessing the performance of partnerships and making recommendations for improvements.

- Managing budgets and resources related to partnerships.

- Staying current on industry trends and developments and incorporating this knowledge into partnerships.

Building and maintaining relationships with industry

- leaders, organizations, and other key stakeholders.

- A successful Strategic Alliance Manager should have strong negotiation, communication, and relationship-building skills and experience in developing and managing partnerships. They should also be knowledgeable about the industry and market trends and be able to effectively manage budgets and resources. A Bachelor's degree in Business, Marketing, or a related field is typically required, and experience in a related role is preferred.

CHAPTER THIRTY

ADDITIONAL RESOURCES

There are several ways to learn more about strategic alliances:

Books:

Several books are available on strategic alliances, such as "Strategic Alliances: An Entrepreneur's Guide to Joint Ventures and Partnerships" by Richard Whiteley.

Online courses:

Online courses such as Coursera and Udemy offer courses on strategic alliances.

Conferences:

Attending conferences on strategic alliances can provide opportunities to network with other professionals and learn about the latest trends and best practices.

Professional organizations:

Joining professional organizations such as the Strategic Alliance Society, Association of Strategic Alliance Professionals and the Alliance Management Professional Society can provide access to resources, networking opportunities, and events focused on the topic.

Case studies:

Studying case studies of successful and failed strategic alliances can provide insights into the complexities of these partnerships and the factors that contribute to their success or failure.

Follow me on Linkedin:
https://www.linkedin.com/in/ericsnethkamp/

Here you'll find information on upcoming posts, articles, conversations, brainstorming sessions, webinars, specific tips, techniques, training, thought leadership and more.

About Author

Eric Snethkamp is a Strategic Alliances & Channels leader with significant experience that spans over 2 decades primarily within the insurance, human capital management, benefits, and technology spaces. He's been recognized in the multiple industries as a strong leader and trusted advisor with demonstrated successes in recruiting, managing, training, and developing top-performing strategic alliance programs and teams. His expertise lies in the design, implementation, execution, and growth of new or restructured strategic alliances & partnerships and is well-versed in developing strategic plans and programs based on company goals that will promote sales growth and customer satisfaction for the organization.

AREAS OF EXPERTISE: Team Leadership | Strategic Alliances & Partnerships | Channel Sales | Client/Customer Success | Business Strategy | Presentations & Proposals | Process Improvement | Revenue Generation | Cost Control | Human Resources | Business Development | Needs Assessment | Program Management | Policy & Procedure Development | Research & Analysis | Budget Management | Public Relations | Negotiation |

www.ingramcontent.com/pod-product-compliance
Lightning Source LLC
Chambersburg PA
CBHW070755220526
45467CB00014B/530